THE BEGINNER GUITARIST
PLAYBOOK
(Tricks that will blow your mind)

By
DEN LÓPEZ

If you want to learn guitar "hands free"

Contents

INTRODUCTION

Welcome to this playbook!

My name is Den Lopez.

I wrote this playbook to help you in your journey. To let you see how easy guitar really is.

Now, like with anything, mastering how to play the guitar will take time. But the amount of time needed will be much less if you know how.

And the learning experience will be far more enjoyable **with all the pieces of the puzzle coming together nicely.**

Let me tell you the story of why I got into teaching guitar.

One afternoon I was practicing some guitar parts on my '96 Mexican Strat and a friend of mine came over to visit.

After seeing me play, she said: Wow! That's so cool! I'm going to sign up my daughter for guitar lessons😊

The first thing that came to my mind was: Oh no! Poor child!

Instantly I knew what that girl was going to go through. The process, the pain, the frustration.

I knew my friend did not know what she was signing her daughter up for.

You've been there. Learning your first chords. Trying to change from one chord to the next fast enough to keep up with the song. The mighty and terrible F chord.

And all this without having a clue of what you are doing!

I also felt like the guitar was a maze where there was too much to learn and no clear direction.

The Beginner
Guitatrist Playbook

I also got frustrated sounding like a beginner for years!

It took me so long to understand how the guitar worked and why my playing did not sound quite "right".

So I started to think about this girl and how I could help her not go through that pain.

I realized that the biggest struggle for beginners is fretting chords and changing through them quickly.

That is when I came up with "The Guitar In 1 Hour Method" which makes complete beginners be able to **play full songs in under an hour.**

When I started putting my ideas out there, I began to see that even guitar teachers admired my method of teaching. So I got addicted to finding tricks, easy wins, and ways to make guitar easy and fun.

This playbook follows the framework I teach my students. All laid out with the diagrams I've shared with them that gave them the best insights. **The ones that helped them the most.**

I left some topics out of this book because I know information overload leads to not taking action. Simplicity is key.

For that reason, this book is structured in a way where every concept weaves and builds on the previous one.

Do not worry if everything doesn't click right away. If you can get one good idea from this book that helps you understand the guitar a bit better, I will consider it a huge win.

Hope you like it and **let's get playing!**

Den López

The Beginner Guitatrist Playbook

But before we start... I want you to have the best playing experience.

That is why I want to give you some tips that might seem obvious, but really help.

Hot Tips!

1. Always tune your guitar before playing.

Yes I know. Of course! But have you tuned your guitar? Playing in tune makes you sound better which makes you play better.

2. Use a lighter string gauge.

Specially with acoustics. They all come with 13's mounted from the factory. And they can be hard on your fingers.

Try 11's, or even 10's!

3. Get a good setup.

The more comfortable your guitar feels, the more you will play it. The more you play it, the better you'll get. The beter you get, the more you'll want to play.

See how it's a vicious cycle on your favour?

A good setup should cost you anywhere from $20 to $50.

Always ask for an estimate and give precise instructions not to go over what you want to pay.

Normally luthiers are good people, but I've heard horror stories.

Let' dig in!

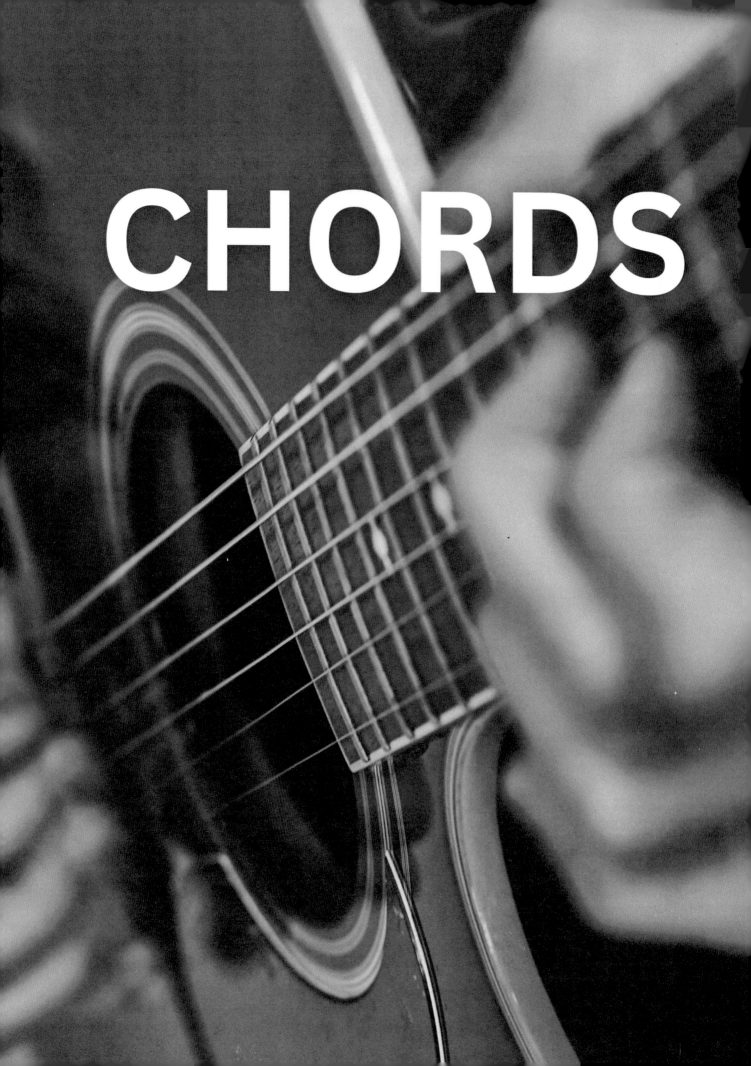

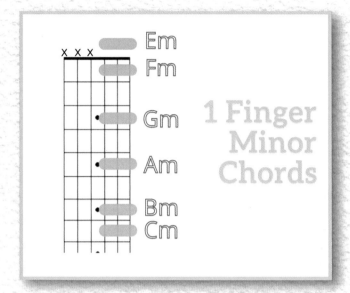

This image blows everyone's mind. Every time.

As beginners, we all struggle with changing chords to be able to play the songs we love.

And then you hit an even higher wall when you try to play barre chords.

You look up a song you're trying to play, and there it is: Bm, or F.

By strumming through the 1st, 2nd, and 3rd strings (the thinnest) without even fretting the guitar, you're playing an E minor chord.

If we treat those open strings as a shape (nut), we can then move that shape across the neck to play any basic minor chord, just with 1 finger.

Note that sharps and flats are not in the diagram for aesthetic reasons, but you can use the same shape to play all simple minor chords.

For example: **F#m would be at the 2nd fret.**

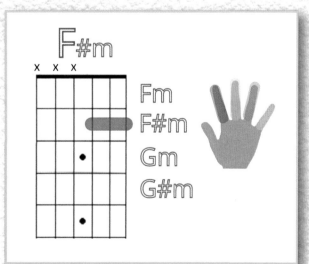

How is it that you can play a full chord by using only 3 strings?

Basic chords are created by playing 3 notes together.

But there are 6 strings on the guitar!

If we want to play all six strings, we must repeat some of those notes.

The best chord shape to illustrate this is the A shape (below).

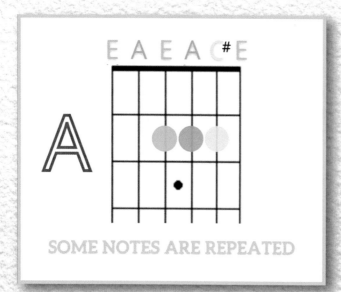

See how the notes on the 6th and 5th strings are **the same notes** as the ones on the 4th and 3rd strings?

The 1st string is also the same note as the 6th and 4th string.

The only note that is not repeated is located on the 2nd string (yellow).

Again, if we treat that chord as a shape, we can move it across the fretboard to **play all the basic major chords.**

We just fret the 1st, 2nd, and 3rd strings to play basic minor chords.

We can also fret the 2nd, 3rd, and 4th strings to create basic major chords.

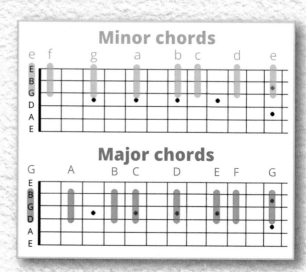

CHORDS VS SHAPES

When you first started playing, you were probably told to learn "chords".

And that is a **dangerous word**, because it makes you believe that chords are "a thing".

If you just use another word you will suddenly understand how the guitar works.

Instead of the word "chords", we are going to use the word "shapes" from now on. **Shapes that create chords.**

Think of it this way.
If you fret 1 single note (5th fret-1st string for example), and then you fret the 6th fret, what happened to that note?
It became another note, correct?

Think of it this way.

If you fret 1 single note (5th fret-1st string for example), and then you fret the 6th fret, what happened to that note?

It became another note, correct?

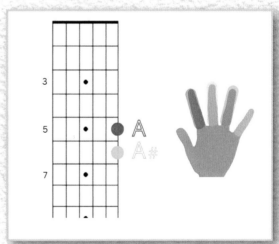

Well, when you play 3 notes together (chord), what do you think will happen if you play that exact shape 1 fret higher?

Exactly, it becomes another chord!

All the notes that make up the chord move up in pitch at the same time.

This means that if you learn a D chord SHAPE, you can slide it across the neck to play all the other major chords.

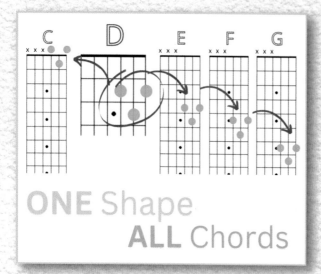

ONE Shape
ALL Chords

It's easier to see this by playing an F chord (below).

Try playing an F chord and then moving it back 1 fret towards the headstock.

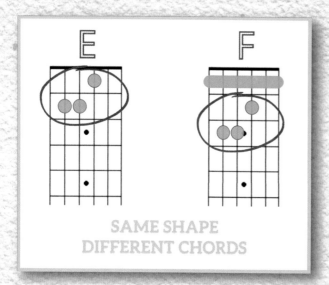

SAME SHAPE
DIFFERENT CHORDS

See how it becomes an E?

This is true for any chord shape.

Try this with the B chord. Even if you can't fret it well yet.

See how if you move it two frets down, towards the headstock, it becomes an A?

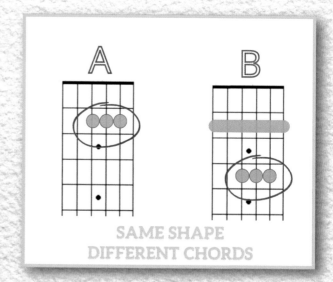

SAME SHAPE
DIFFERENT CHORDS

Now you know that **you can move any chord shape across the fretboard to create any o chord.**

The whole neck is available to you now.

For example, if you want to play an F chord, you can use the E shape and move it 1 fret higher, towards the bridge.

And 2 frets higher from that to play a G chord.

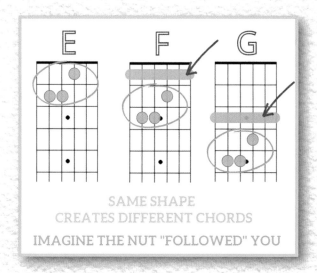

SAME SHAPE
CREATES DIFFERENT CHORDS
IMAGINE THE NUT "FOLLOWED" YOU

Any chord shape is movable!

You can also move a **D shape 3 frets higher to play an F too.**

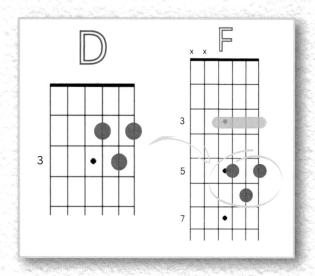

Or a **C shape and move it up 5 frets!**

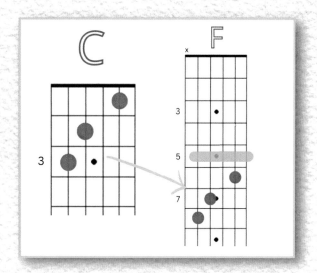

There are 5 major chord shapes that we use to create all the other chords.

You might have heard of them as open chords. But remember, from now on, you are going to think of them as shapes.

13

They are the **C** shape, the **A** shape, the **G** shape, the **E** shape, and the **D** shape.

Hence, the word: **C - A - G - E - D**

Hopefully, you now understand that the open chords you learned when starting out are not really chords.

They are **shapes that create chords.**

And that you can move those shapes across the neck to create other chords.

Now, here comes the tricky part.

If you want to play all 6 strings, **you have to make all 6 string change in pitch at the same time.**

If you move an E shape 1 fret higher, there are some strings left behind that do not change in pitch.

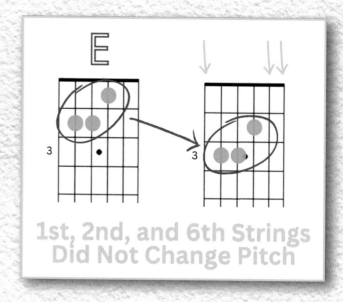

1st, 2nd, and 6th Strings Did Not Change Pitch

But you can move them, following the chord shape, with what we call a **barre**.

Imagine the nut of the guitar was your index finger.

Now you have a movable nut to follow any chord shape you want to play.

That is why they are called barre chords. They are just "chord shapes" with a "barre" behind them.

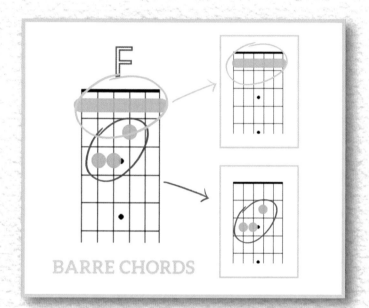

Look at this diagram.

An F chord can be broken down into its **"chord shape"** (circled in red) and the **"barre"** itself (circled in green).

The same happens with any barre chord.

For example the most common way of playing a Bm chord (using the Am chord shape).

Again the chord shape is circled in red and the barre in green.

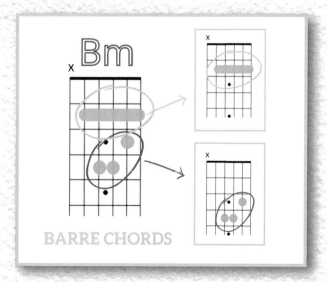

15

Barre chords can be tricky to fret and it can be even more challenging to change quickly from open chord shapes to barre chords.

We go deep into how to make them easy to play inside the PERFECT BARRE CHORDS course.

If you're struggling with barre chords, check it out!

Let me give you a couple of tips anyway.

Hot tips to play barre chords:

- Always fret your strings as close to the fret wire as possible (this is true for anything you fret, not just chords).
- Get your guitar set up by a professional.
- Practice at the 3rd fret instead of at the first.

Instead of placing your index finger in the middle of the fret, **try moving it as close to the fret wire as possible.**

Not on top of the fret wire, just very close.

There are more tricks and tips we cover inside the course for example:

If you're still having trouble making all 6 strings ring clearly, **try this:**

Place a capo behind the barre chord you're trying to play.

It will bring the strings closer so you don't have to press as hard.

Let's look at how you can turn 3 of those open "shapes" into 18 different chords.

We are going to be focusing on the **E**, the **A**, and the **D** shape.

What's cool about these 3 chord shapes is that they share the same structure.

With that, I mean the notes that create them are placed in the same order.

You probably know the notes of those strings already, because of your tuner.

E A D G B E

Turn 3 chords into 18!

To turn any one of those shapes into a 7th chord, move the note on the **middle fretted string (red)** down 2 frets towards the headstock.

For example the **E shape:**

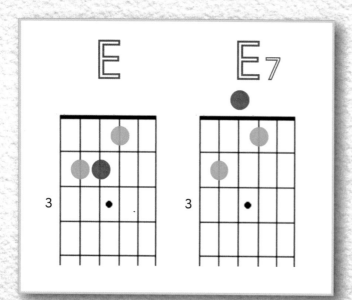

The middle fretted string is the 4th string for the E shape.

Move it down two frets and you have an E7 chord.

Easy.

The same thing applies to the A and D shapes.

The middle fretted string for the A shape is the 3rd string.

If you move it down 2 frets you have an A7 chord.

The middle fretted string for the D shape is the 2nd string.

Exactly the same principle.

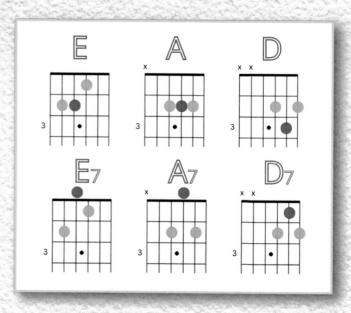

To turn these shapes into **maj7 chords,** use the same string but move it just **one fret** towards the headstock.

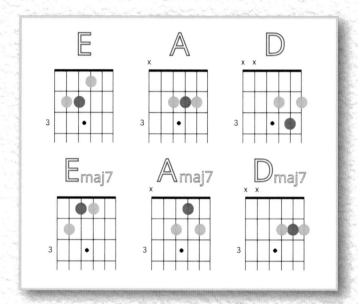

Again we use the middle fretted string for each chord shape.

But we move it just one fret lower to create maj7 chords.

Easy.

Now let's turn those shapes into minor chords.

To do this, take the *thinnest string* you're fretting (green) and move it 1 fret down towards the headstock.

For example, **an E turns into an Em like this.**

The same thing applies to the A and D shapes.

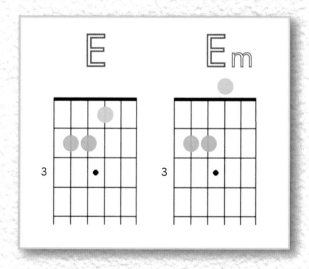

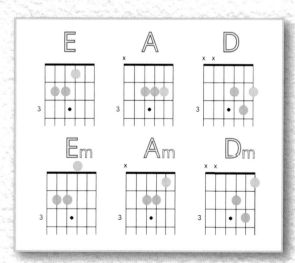

What's cool is that **you can combine both tricks together.**

So, if you want to turn an E into an Em7...

You move the thinnest fretted string (green) 1 fret towards the headstock, and the middle fretted string (red), 2 frets towards the headstock.

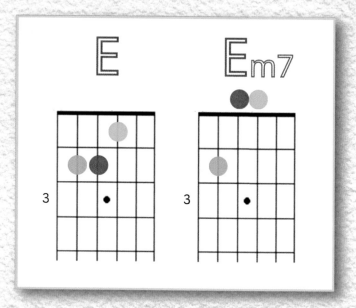

The same thing happens with the A and D shapes if we wanted to transform them into minor 7th chords.

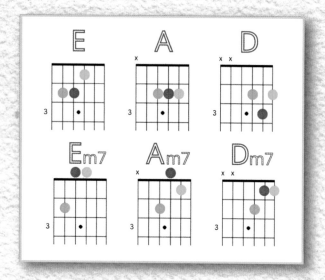

So now, with 3 shapes, you have...

18 chords!

But remember, you can play any chord you want with any one of these "open shapes", just by sliding them across the fretboard and placing a barre behind it!

To find where those chords are, we use the thickest 3 strings as a reference.

Remember those strings are tuned to E (6th), A (5th), D (4th).

Using the E shape

To use the E shape to play any chord, we use the sixth string (E string).

You just need to find the note of the chord you want to play, and **that is where you place your barre**.

Then you can use any form of the E shape chord to play the chord you want.

Here are the notes on the 6th string (remember, the E string).

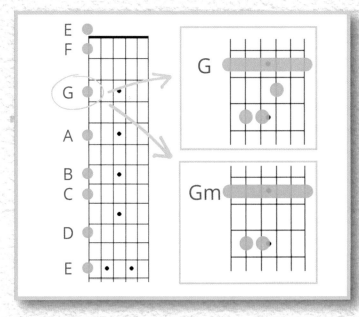

So, for instance, let's say you want to play a G or a Gm.

You can see that to play a G major chord, you use the E major shape.

To play a Gm chord, you use the Em shape.

But you can use any E shape to play any chord!

To play a G7, just place your barre at the 3 fret and use an E7 shape in front of it.

21

Using the A shape

To use the A shape to play any chord, **we use the 5th string** (A string).

Look for the note of the chord you want to play and place your barre there.

Then use any A shape you want and boom! There is your chord. Here are the notes on the 5th strings (remember, the A string).

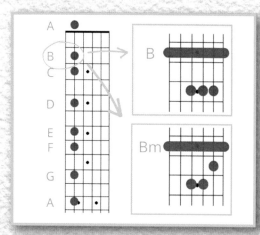

Say you want to play B or Bm.

Just look for the B note. Your barre goes there.

Then use an A major shape to play B, and an Am shape to play Bm.

Using the D shape

This works the same way with the D shape, **using the 4th string.** Here are the notes on the 4th string (remember, the D string).

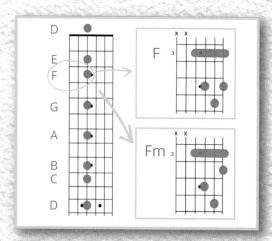

To play an F or an F minor, just look for the F note on the 4th string.

Then use the D major shape to play F or the D minor shape to play Fm.

Now, trying to barre a D shape across the neck is a big stretch... which is why the E and A shapes are the most commonly used.

But you don't have to play all 6 strings all the time!

You can choose to play 3, 4, 5, or even just 1.

There are no rules. If you choose to use only 3 strings to play basic chords you are playing **TRIADS**.

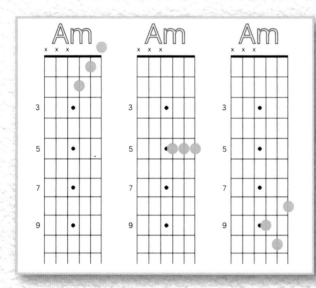

You probably recognize the shape use to play Am on the right hand side of the diagram.

Exactly!

A Dm shape.

Triad meaning 3 notes.

3 notes that if you remember from the first diagram, **create a basic chord.**

This diagram shows how a "full chord shape" can be broken down into triads.

For extra points: What chord shape are we using to play this Am chord?

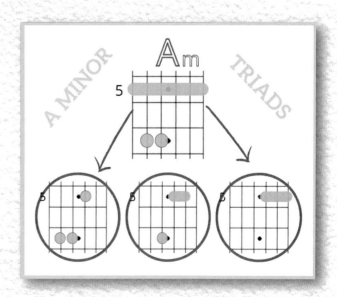

Take a look at this other diagram:

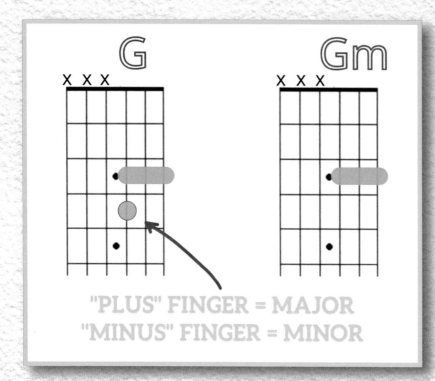

To change from a minor chord (triad) to a major, **we only need to change one note!**

Like when we transformed the E, A, and D chord shapes into minor chords, we just moved 1 note.

This means we can play any simple chord with our index and middle fingers.

And you might be asking yourself...Why do I need to know this?

If you ever want to play Reggae for example, these are the chords to go to.

Watch any recording of Marley and you'll see him playing chords like this.

There are other cool things you can do with triads as well (solos, cool intros, recording a second guitar in a recording...) Tons of amazing stuff.

For now, just know that if you're struggling to play a Bm, you can pull it off by fretting the thinnest 3 strings at the 7th fret.

Here's an example using triads to **play arpeggios for song intros.**

For this example, let's imagine your song starts with the chords G - Bm - Em. Using the 1st, 2nd, and 3rd strings.

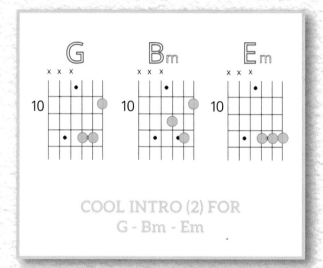

Or another example: This time using the 2nd, 3rd, and 4th strings.

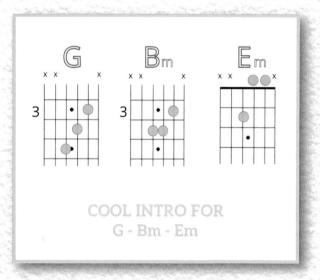

For extra points!

What shapes are used to play a Bm in both diagrams?

You can play really cool intros by just plucking on each string individually.

If you want more on this, check out the Triads For Beginners course.

Let's talk about some easy chord changes next.

Easy Chord Changes

There are many chords that share shapes, or that involve minimal finger changes, giving you the chance to **switch from one to the other quickly.**

For example: Am to C

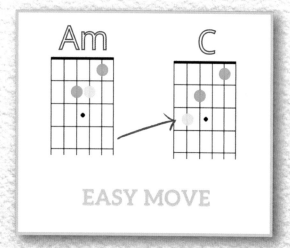

EASY MOVE

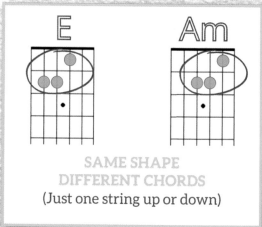

SAME SHAPE
DIFFERENT CHORDS
(Just one string up or down)

You see it's only one finger (ring finger) that you have to move.

The others stay at the same place, or "locked".

Another example is Am to E, where the chord shape is exactly the same, but bounces strings.

Like in the image to your right.

Same happens with this other example: Em to Asus2.

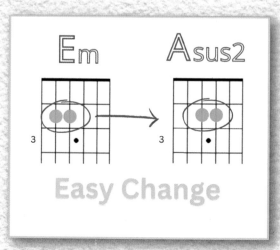

Easy Change

You can find all kinds of hidden shared shapes between chords. For example: **Am to Dm** (below).

Quick tip:

If you're an older player and you find it hard fretting a Dm, many of my students find it easier playing it like this:

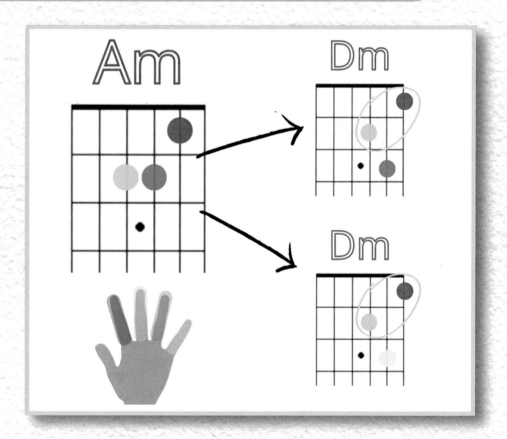

Sometimes your fingers just won't stretch as much as you would like. Using your pinky finger might be easier for you.

Now let's transition to how you can start sounding amazing!

RHYTHM

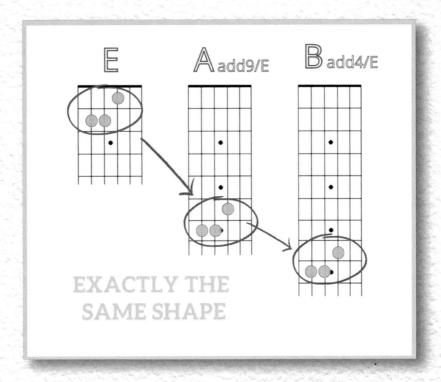

So many times we get caught up in trying to become better players by perfecting our fretting hand technique.

You focus most of your attention on your "chord hand" because that's what they taught you to do first.

Here is the HARD truth: **Perfecting your rhythm hand is what will make you sound like an experienced guitarist.**

Not how well you fret chords or how fast you change from one to the next.

That is why I posted the diagram above. So you don't even have to think about changing chords, and you can focus exclusively on rhythm.

I struggled with this for years, always sounding like a beginner, no matter how hard I tried.

It took forever to discover this: **Rhythm is the key.**

If you take away anything from this book, let it be this:

TAKE WHAT YOU ALREADY KNOW, AND APPLY RHYTHM TO IT.

It is that simple.

I can't tell you how many people who after taking my rhythm course wrote back to me saying how much better they sounded, immediately.

Not only that, but they were amazed at how much easier it was to change through chords.

Rhythm is what brings everything together.

With rhythm, **anything you play will sound like music, even if it's just one chord.**

Put it this way: Imagine you and I meet to jam with my band.

You play rhythm and I'll play lead guitar.

We can jam for hours over one single chord as long as you're playing in time.

We might get bored after a while, but we're playing music.

It might be simple, but it's music.

Now let's say you play 3 chords but your rhythm is not in place. Now suddenly everything falls apart.

The drummer can't follow you, the bass player gets mad and leaves... It's a mess.

The same thing happens if you're playing on your own. **You can sense it.**

Which brings me to this image.

Don't let anyone put that idea in your head. **IT IS NOT TRUE.**

I have yet to find someone that cannot count to 4 in time.
The problem comes with fear.

Changing from a C to a D as a beginner is HUGE.

It requires all of your attention which then is taken away from the rhythm hand.

And **that is why you sound like a beginner for so long**. Because you can sense there is something off.

Here are some cool and **easy chord changes** that won't require your full attention.

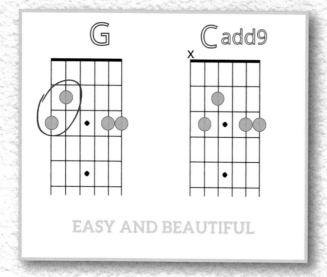

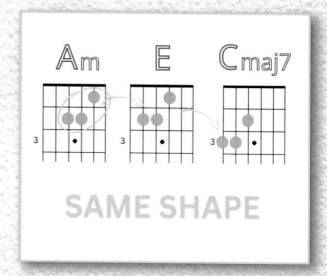

When playing this, note that your index and middle finger use the same "shape".

They just jump strings.

By moving this shape through the strings you can play a three chord progression that sounds amazing.

Here's another example you can explore:

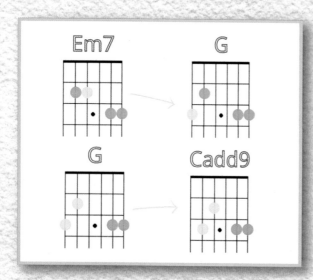

Lock down your pinky and ring fingers at the 1st and 2nd string.

Notice that the notes represented in yellow are the ones that move position.

The blue ones stay locked in the same place.

If you're struggling to move from a C to an F **try this instead:**

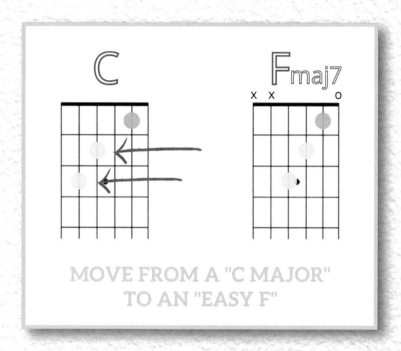

MOVE FROM A "C MAJOR"
TO AN "EASY F"

This "cheat F" works great as a substitute on many songs.
To go from a C to an Fmaj7 move your middle and ring fingers one string.

An easy way to do this is by visualizing those two notes as a shape.

Here's a **quote by Cory Wong,**master rhythm guitarist from the band Vulfpeck:

"...the right hand, once you get the motor down, makes things pretty easy"

And it's true. Your rhythm hand is "your engine".

Keep it moving all the time, even if you're not playing.

33

Now, I know you might feel intimidated when you see something like this:

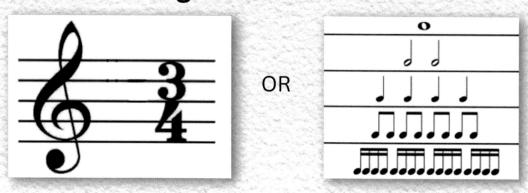

OR

Or when you hear things like "quarter note" or "eighth note", because you've been taught using theory, instead of with practice.

But rhythm is a lot more simple than it looks.

Let's say you see 3/4.

That just means you count to three.

You can simply forget about the bottom number and focus on the top number.

It just means you strum three times, and repeat.

If you see a 4/4, you just strum 4 times and repeat.

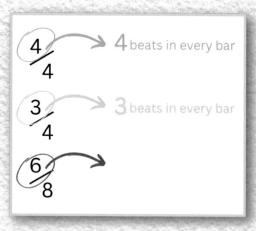

If the top number is 3, you count to three. If the top number is 4, you count to four.

And if it's 6? You guessed it. Forget the bottom number for now.

Let's imagine they tell you a song is in 4/4.

That just means you're counting 4 beats, or units in time.

Those 4 beats are grouped into a **bar**, or a small segment of music.

Multiple beats make up a bar, and multiple bars make up a part of a song.

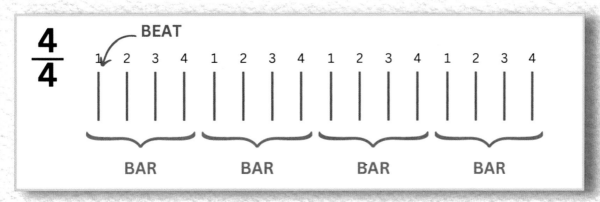

For example,
In a song we all know:

HOTEL CALIFORNIA

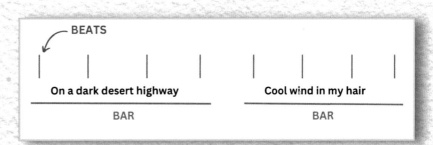

The easiest way to get this right is to **start simple.**

Just play a down strum for every beat. Yup. Nothing wrong with that.

And do it **VERY slowly**.
The slower, the more time you'll have.

SCAN ME! »

That way you'll have time to change chords.

It will still sound like music. Maybe slow music, but music after all.

If you strum in slow motion you'll notice that to play the next down strum, your hand has to come up.

This means we could potentially play an "up strum" in between each "down strum".

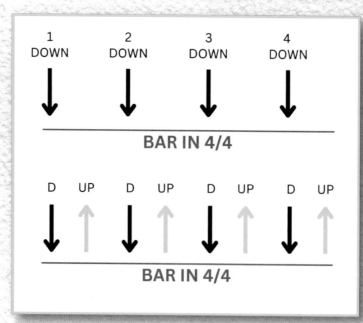

Now we have 8 strums: *4 down strums* and *4 up strums*.

And it's time to play around with them, creating **strumming patterns.**

Inside 'The Most Important Thing' rhythm course for beginners I teach something I call:

'THE CIRCLE OR ERASE METHOD'

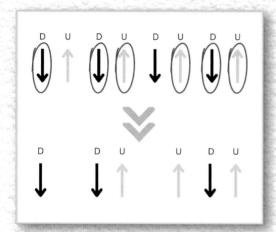

If you draw those strums on a piece of paper, you can circle the ones you want to play and come up with any variation you wish.

Just strum the ones you circled and avoid the rest.

Doing it on a whiteboard, you can erase the strums you don't want to play. **Hence, The Circle or Erase Method.**

Again, I can't stress enough how important rhythm is. It is the key to sounding great.

If you don't get it right, you will never sound legit.

The good thing is, **rhythm is the easiest thing to learn.** A lot easier than chords.

Look at this definition of rhythm.

Rhythm: Music's pattern in time. Whatever other elements a given piece of music may have (e.g., patterns in pitch or timbre), rhythm is the one indispensable element of all music. Rhythm can exist without melody, as in the drumbeats of so-called primitive music, **but melody cannot exist without rhythm.**

Basically said...
Music is not music without rhythm.

Once your rhythm is in place, and you know a couple of basic chord shapes (remember you can slide those shapes across the fretboard), you can play 1000's of songs.

So many people find it difficult to play full songs but it's very simple.

Remember when they made you learn a poem by heart at school?

And then they made you stand in front of the class and recite it?

I remember one in particular by Robert Frost. "The Road Not Taken". Great poem btw.

You had to learn every line, correct?

What happened when you forgot a line?

Everything fell apart. You might have remembered the line after that, but if you got stuck on one, you couldn't continue.

And you ended up with a D on your report card.

That is how most people approach learning songs: By memorizing every single line.

But songs don't work that way.

Almost any song you'll want to play can be broken down into parts that are repeated over and over.

The two most important parts are usually: The **VERSE** and the **CHORUS**.

There are other parts that you might see. Such as: INTRO, OUTRO, BRIDGE...

Here's an example of a song you probably know "Oh! Susanna"

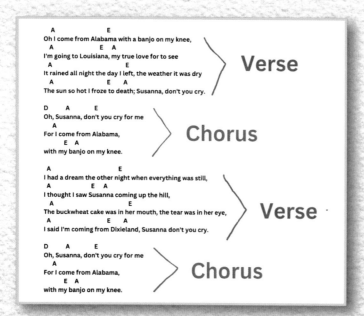

As you can see, the whole song can be divided into two parts: **VERSES** and **CHORUS**.

The great thing about this is that each verse structure is exactly the same.

And each chorus structure is exactly the same as well.

Now you only have to learn 2 things, instead of memorizing the whole poem.

But, and this also happens with many songs, **look even closer at the verse.**

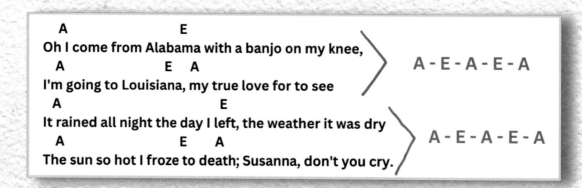

It repeats itself too!

Verse 1 is divided into A E A E A (x2).

This means you only have to learn that sequence and play it two times per verse.

Now, instead of having to memorize a full poem, you just have to learn a couple of lines.

To quickly find songs that you can play right now, you can choose to **filter songs by chords.**

To do this, head over to **The Chord Genome Project** and filter songs by the chords you feel most comfortable playing.

With just 3 chords, you'll be able to play 1000s of songs.

If you know 4 chords, 10s of thousands.

REALLY.

Speaking of songs, **would you like to write your own songs?**

So many times we don't do things because we have fear of failing.

With this method, failing is not a possibility.

Check this out:

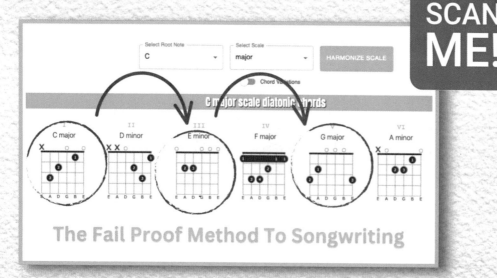

This website lets you harmonize any chord.

Just enter a chord and choose either major or minor.

It will give you **all the chords that work well around that original chord.**

If you start by playing a C chord, you can follow it by playing any one of these other chords: Dm, Em, F, G, or Am.

In whatever order you want. Literally.

You can try C- F - Dm - Am. Fantastic!

Or how about C - Em - G - C. Sounds beautiful!

And the cool thing is that you can do it for any chord. Major or minor.

Try writing your own verses and choruses! Same as with Oh! Susanna!

You can become a songwriter today.

One last thing about playing songs...

Have you ever searched for a song you wanted to play and fancy chords show up?

Chords you have no idea how to play?

Take for example "Don't Let Me Down" by The Beatles.

The chords in the song are: F - Gm7 - C - C7

But you don't have to play it exactly like the Beatles did.

You can play F - Gm - C and **it will still sound pretty close.**

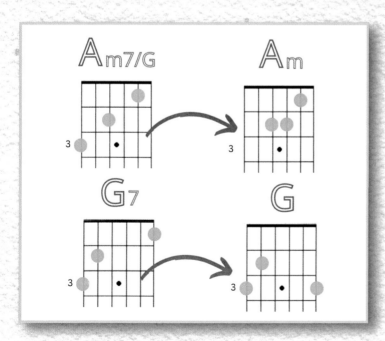

Do not let fancy names intimidate you or keep you from playing the songs you love.

Next time you see a G7, and you don't know how to play it, just play a G.

It's that simple.

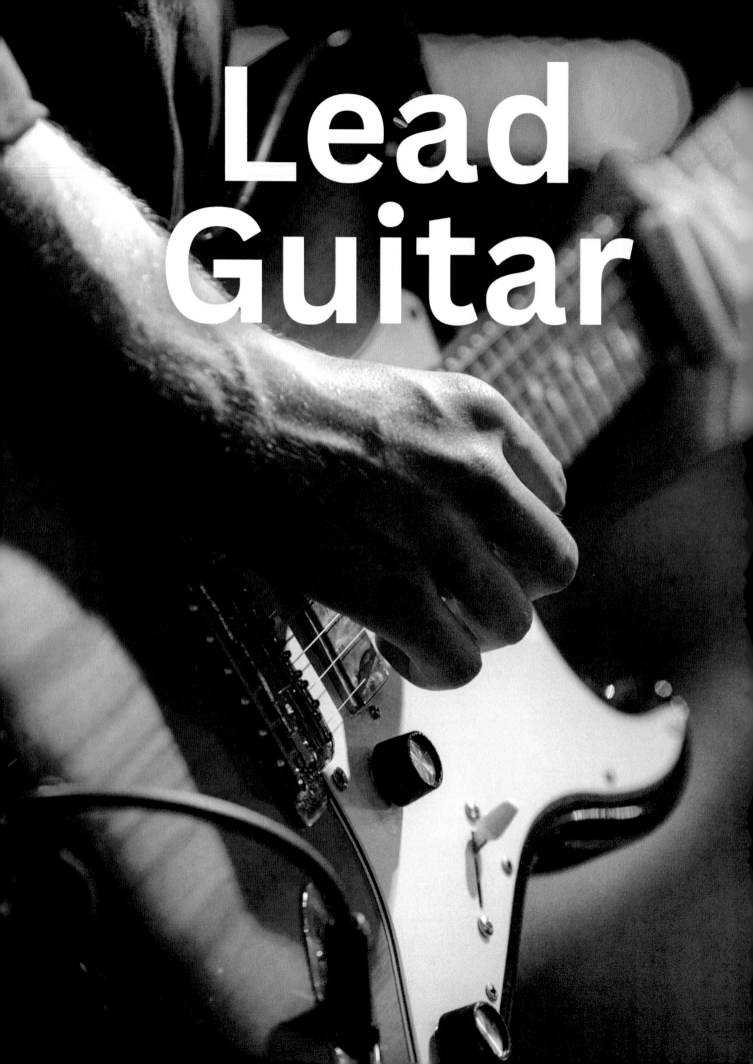

Lead
Guitar

Lead guitar has to be one of the most enjoyable things to do with the guitar.

I compare playing lead to singing. **It is a way to express yourself.**

When I teach my students how to start playing lead, I only let them play one note. Yup, just one.

We start with one note for a reason.

I hear so many people play at blazing speeds, all across the neck, a million notes per minute, but they say nothing with their playing.

If you compare a single note to a single letter, it's very different to say *"ah"* like a robot (which means nothing) to screaming *AHHHHHHH* at the top of your lungs.

Same as it will sound very different if you add a question mark at the end "a".

By screaming a note, you might be demanding attention or expressing danger.

By adding a question mark at the end of that note, you might be expressing doubt, or confusion.

Same note, different feelings.

By focusing on one note, you can really be intentional about what you are trying to say with it.

You can bend it, slide up or down to it, do a hammer-on, a pull-off, apply vibrato…

Even play it on different beats, or for different lengths of time. You can hit it hard or soft.

All this affects what you're trying to say with your instrument.

A diagram with just one note would be silly, so I teach my students this, second.

Just four notes.

In this diagram the A minor box is represented.

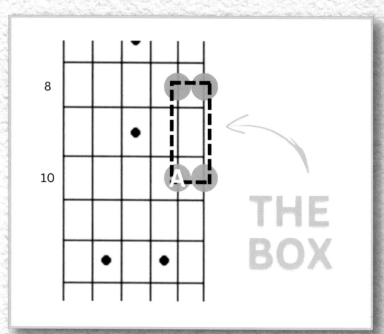

THE BOX

There is so much music you can play with these four notes.

Plus, it's four of the five notes of the "Pentatonic Scale" (Penta meaning 5).

To complete the pentatonic scale you just need to add one more note, and turn "The Box" into "The House".

Also called **"The House Of Blues"** because:

1. It's shaped like a house.

2. Every great blues guitar player lives there.

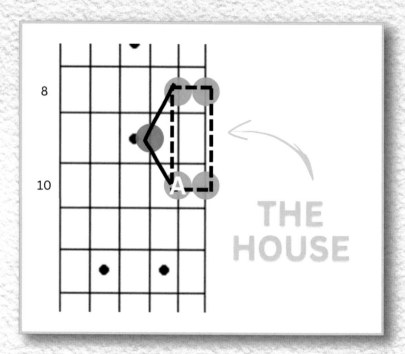

THE HOUSE

SCAN ME! »

Let me show you how the fretboard works, and how you can **use the box to play over all 6 strings, across 8 frets.**

There are many ways to memorize the fretboard.

You might be looking down at your guitar and thinking: How on earth am I supposed to memorize every note?

How can you navigate the fretboard and not get lost?

This is the way I teach my students: **"The Two-String Approach".**

This approach is not meant to be a definite way to learn every single note (although if you know the notes on any pair of strings you can find them on the others).

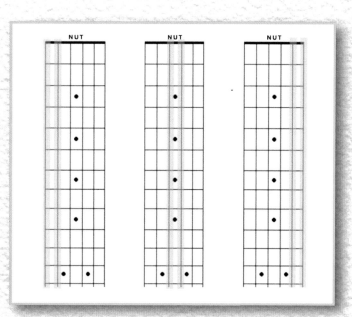

It's just meant to **simplify and make the guitar less abstract.**

Less intimidating in a way.

You can divide all 6 strings into 3 pairs: The 6th and 5th, the 4th and 3rd, and the 2nd and 1st.

Whatever you find on the 6th and 5th strings, will be repeated in exactly the same order on the other pairs of strings.

You just need to bounce frets.

So let's say you find two notes on the thickest two strings (6th and 5th).

To find the same notes on the 4th and 3rd strings, **you just have to move 2 frets higher.**

To find them on the 2nd and 1st strings, **you move 3 frets higher from there.**

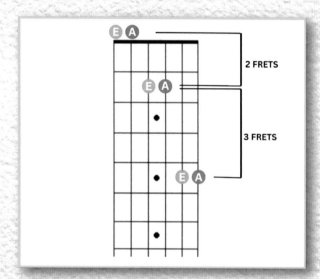

Now, remember that little box you learned on the 2nd and 1st strings?

Because the guitar repeats itself over every pair of strings, **we can find the box again on the 4th and 3rd strings, and on the 6th and 5th.**

Below you have a diagram where every note in the box is colored so you can see how the notes are the same in every pair of strings, and follow the same sequence.

This means that if you learn a little lick or run on a pair of strings, you can play the same lick on all the other strings!

The same exact lick.

Pretty nice, right?

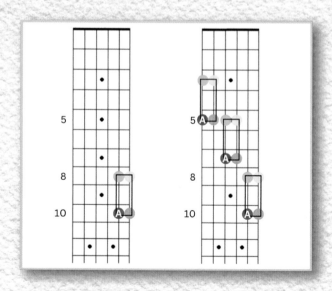

To join all three boxes you need that extra note that makes this a full pentatonic run.

Remember however, **it's only 5 notes that repeat themselves.**

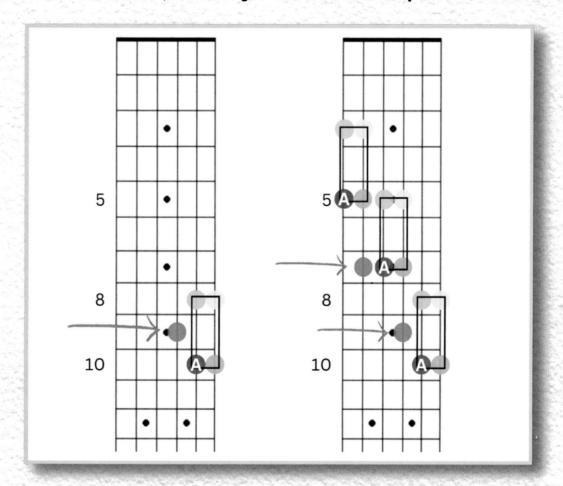

You might be confused not seeing "The House" repeated again.

That is because to play "The House" shape we use 3 strings, not 2.

Look at the purple note that turns "The Box" into "The House" on the 3rd string.

See how you can find the same note, two frets, down on the other pair of strings?

You can also play these 5 notes *vertically* instead of *horizontally*.

We call this "scale positions", and the most common one is **position 1.**

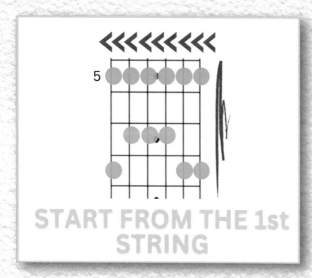

START FROM THE 1st STRING

Everyone learns scales starting from the 6th string, but **no one starts solos at the 6th string!**

So, what I recommend you do is **learn scales starting from the 1st string.**

That way you won't have to mentally run up the scale to find where you want to start.

In the image above, you see the minor pentatonic scale position 1 in the key of A.

The cool thing about position 1 is that **half the scale is already done for you.**

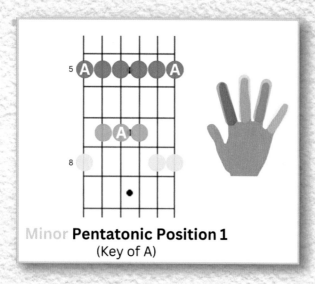

Minor **Pentatonic Position 1**
(Key of A)

As you can see, **half the scale lies on the same fret** (fret 5 for A minor).

Now you only need to know the other half.

You can use any fingers you want, but **if you want to play it fast**, you can use 1 finger per fret.

But let's say you want to play in the key of B, or in any other key.

Remember how "chord shapes" can be moved across the fretboard to create other chords?

The same thing happens with "scale shapes".

To play in another key, you just have to move your scale shape across the fretboard.

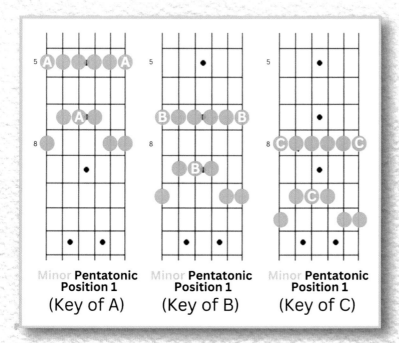

Minor **Pentatonic Position 1**
(Key of A)

Minor **Pentatonic Position 1**
(Key of B)

Minor **Pentatonic Position 1**
(Key of C)

So, starting with the A minor pentatonic, we would move that shape two frets higher (towards the bridge) to play in the key of B.

One fret higher from there to play in the key of C.

Two frets higher from there, to play in the key of D.

Do you see the pattern? Like with chord shapes, it follows the alphabet:

A B C D E F G...

It's always the same: Follow the alphabet.

The reason everyone teaches the "minor pentatonic" scale first, is because it works great with both major and minor chord progressions (generally speaking).

The same doesn't happen with the major pentatonic scale. It only works over major chord progressions (again, generally speaking).

But, **what is the key of a song or of a chord progression?**

The key of a song refers to the note or chord a song revolves around. Think of it as home.

You can **find the key of a song by looking at the chord it starts with**, most of the time.

So if a song starts in C, usually, it will be a song in the key of C. If it starts with Gm, usually it will be a song in the key of Gm.

Major scales and chord progressions have a "happier" sound to them, while minor scales and chord progressions sound a bit more "melancholic".

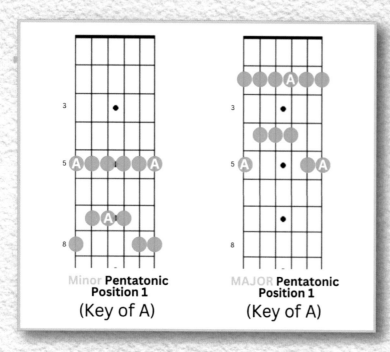

Minor **Pentatonic**
Position 1
(Key of A)

MAJOR **Pentatonic**
Position 1
(Key of A)

To easily **turn minor scales into major scales:**

Just play the same scale shape, 3 frets lower (towards the headstock).

It's that easy.

Caution

Many people get confused by this.

The **scale shape is the same**, but **the notes are not**, nor are they located in the same place.

Look at the minor box and the major box in the same image (in the key of A).

You can see how the root note (the key, or home) **is in the opposite corner of the box.**

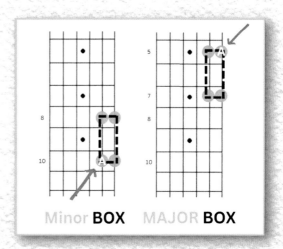

Minor **BOX**   MAJOR **BOX**

So, to recap, **you can play minor scales over any chord progression** and they will sound great most of the time.

To turn those scales into major scales, you just play the same scale shape, 3 frets lower.

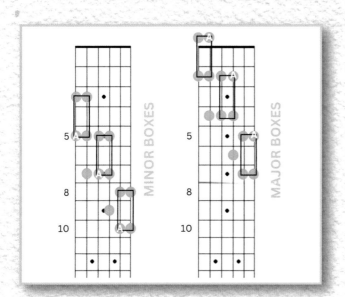

MINOR BOXES   MAJOR BOXES

If you want to change keys, you just follow the alphabet.

A B C D E F G

And it starts again.

If you combine position 1 and position 5 of the pentatonic scale, you find what John Mayer calls...

"The Pentatonic Equator"

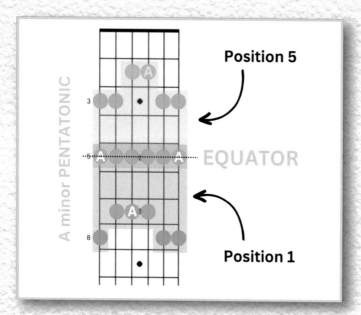

The end of position 5 marks the beginning of position 1, and all those notes are located in the same fret, hence the term equator.

You can use it as a reference to bounce from one position to the other.

Look closely at the diagram for this little trick: On strings 1 through 4 the scale shapes are opposite of each other.

On the 1st and 2nd strings, there are 3 frets on position 1, and 2 frets on position 5.

On the 3rd and 4th strings, there are 2 frets on position 1, and 3 frets on position 5.

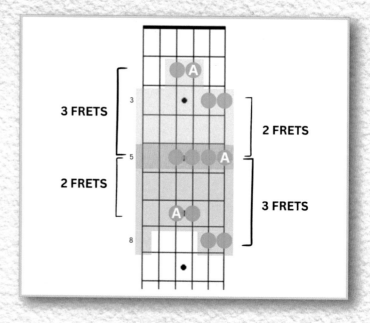

Pentatonic scales are just "broken down" or "simplified" versions of their bigger sisters.

To complete these scales we just need two more notes, turning them into a 7-note scale.

When we introduce these two notes into the major pentatonic, we get the MAJOR scale (7 notes).

Same as with the minor pentatonic. We get a natural MINOR scale.

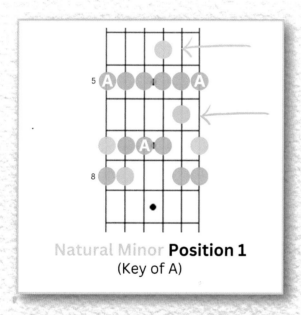

Natural Minor **Position 1**
(Key of A)

In this diagram you can see the two notes that were "missing".

The minor pentatonic scale is represented in blue.

You just need to add two more notes (yellow and green).

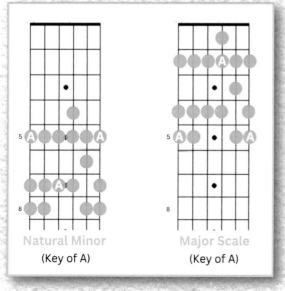

Natural Minor
(Key of A)

Major Scale
(Key of A)

To turn the natural MINOR scale into the MAJOR scale, remember you just need to play the same shape, 3 frets lower.

The Holy Grail

Here comes the fun stuff. Ready???

We can associate scale shapes to chord shapes, and the scale shape will move with it's corresponding chord shape.

In the diagram below you can see the **minor pentatonic scale (red) under the Em chord shape (blue).**

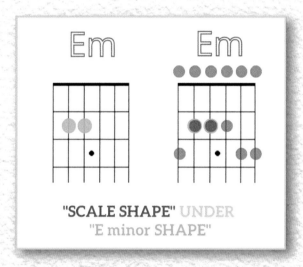

"SCALE SHAPE" UNDER
"E minor SHAPE"

Following the alphabet:
E - F - G...

The scale shape will always follow that chord shape.

So any time you play this shape, you can play the exact same scale under it!

Check out why this is so cool.

In the diagram above, we are playing an Em chord.

If we wanted to play a Gm, we would slide that "chord shape" three frets towards the bridge.

Placing a barre behind it, correct?

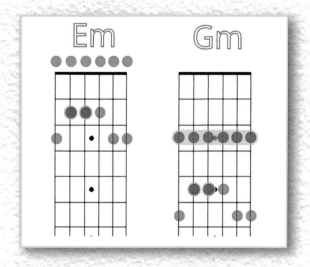

57

The same thing happens with all chord shapes.

You can learn any scale under every chord shape.

Let's stick to pentatonic scales.

Take a look at the Am chord shape to the right.

Remember we can move that shape around?

Let's say you want to play a Bm.

You move that chord shape 2 frets higher and you have a Bm chord.

The scale shape also moves with the chord shape.

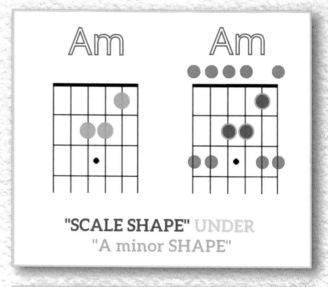

"SCALE SHAPE" UNDER
"A minor SHAPE"

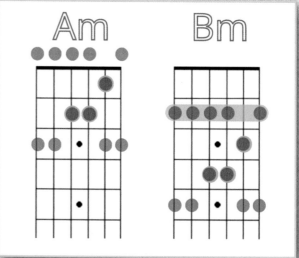

If you learn a little lick or run around this shape, you can play that exact lick every time you use this chord shape and it will sound fantastic!

No matter if you're playing a Cm, Dm, F#m... Whenever you use the "Am chord shape", the scale shape under it will be the same.

You can essentially **combine rhythm and lead guitar in one**.

Many great guitarists have used this approach: Jimi Hendrix, John Mayer, Cornell Dupree...

To practice this, I teach my students to **stay focused on one chord shape.**

Learn the scale shape under that chord and find some cool licks to play around it. Then use the same chord shape to play a chord progression, **playing the same licks over every chord change.**

When I heard I had to learn every scale position in every key, it felt like a huge mountain to climb.

By learning a couple of scale shapes under your chord shapes, you can play really cool guitar without memorizing every scale in every key.

If you try this, you will also find out quickly that chord shapes share scale shapes.

For example, the Am chord shape and the C chord shape. If you look closely, you will start seeing those chords inside the scale shapes.

Look at these diagrams with the pentatonic scales under "open chord shapes"

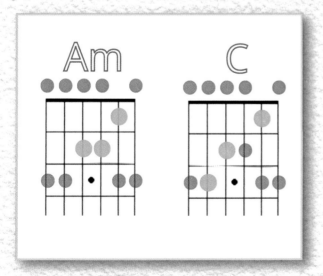
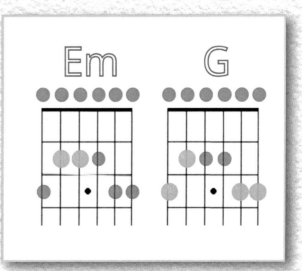

The Beginner
Guitarist Roadmap

To finish up this book, I would love to share with you the framework I teach my students to take them all the way from beginners, to great guitar players.

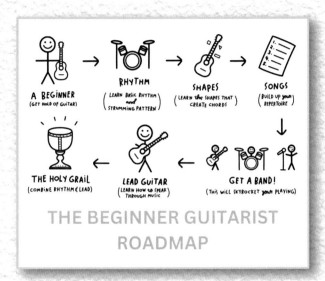

THE BEGINNER GUITARIST ROADMAP

As you can see, **it all starts with rhythm.**

We already discussed how important rhythm is.

If you're struggling to sound legit, probably your rhythm is not in place.

Focus on rhythm, and you'll see how anything you play makes sense.

I met a guy once that played an entire set of 10 songs with just 3 chords. And he managed to pull it off because his rhythm was fantastic.

Second step in the roadmap is changing your mindset around chords. **Change your wording from chords to shapes.**

Shapes that create chords, and can be moved across the fretboard to play any chord.

For example: Let's imagine you are grabbing a guitar for the first time.

With a D chord shape, you can play any major chord by moving that shape across the fretboard.

You could play 1000s of songs!

Turn it into a Dm shape, and now you can play any major or minor chord.

You could play 99% of all songs ever written.

Is this the traditional way of learning how to play? Definitely not. But it gets you playing music immediately.

Not only that, it helps you understand how the guitar works.

The **third step** of this framework is **learning songs.**

This is a huge milestone to reach for beginners. And, most of the time, this is what you really want, right?

Being able to play a song from beginning to end is a great feeling.

Songs are meant to tell stories, to deliver emotion, and to create memories.

Use the tips I showed you to quickly build up your repertoire and play for the people you love.

The **fourth step** in the roadmap is **playing with a band.**
This could also mean playing along to another musician, even if it's not in a band situation.

I recommend to my students that they jam with someone that is way better than them.

It will make you grow fast!

The connection you feel playing with other people is very hard to describe.

You have to experience it to know how it feels.

If you can't find anyone to play with, you can always play to backing tracks. Better than nothing.

But playing with someone is the *real deal.*

The **fifth step** of this framework is **playing lead.**

Think of it as singing. Maybe you sing, maybe you don't. But singing is magical.

There's a reason why most songs are sung. As humans, it is something we like.

Playing lead guitar gives you a chance to get close to that feeling we all love.

Plus, it's extremely fun.

Remember the goal is always to express yourself and deliver emotion. You want to transmit what you're feeling with every note you play.

That is why I teach my students to **start small, with little vocabulary, but great intention.**

And finally, T**he Holy Grail.**

Being able to play lead and rhythm together.

By understanding that shapes create chords, and associating scales shapes under those chord shapes, it's possible to combine both things together.

You don't need to know every scale shape under every chord. **You can pull this off by just knowing a couple.**

Conclusion

I hope this book has helped you understand how the guitar works and continues to help you along your journey.

To finish I would like to **tell you a story of belief**. Of belief in one's self.

When I first started playing, one of my favorite bands was Led Zeppelin, of course!

I used to think only guitar gods could play Stairway To Heaven. But then one day I met a friend that started playing guitar around the same time as I did.

We were talking about music stuff and I said to him: **Imagine if one day we could play Stairway...**

He was like: Oh yeah! I can!

Yeah right! I said to him, in your dreams.

And then the most amazing thing happened. He played it!

Note for note! The whole song! Without stopping!

That day my whole perspective changed.

It gave me the belief that if he could do it, I could too.

After all, he had been playing for as long as I had, and **I was still stuck on chords.**

So we went to a copy shop nearby, made a copy of his tab book, and I ran home.

And sure thing, I started learning Stairway To Heaven.

And I did!

To this day I still remember most of it.

I tell you this story so you take into account that every great guitar player also started out knowing nothing about guitar.

And they also hit walls and went through obstacles, but pushed through.

It's just a matter of belief. **Sometimes it's a little change that changes it all.**

In your hand you have a tool to express yourself. It's just that, a tool.

I'll let you go with these two images.

You got this!

Happy playing!

One last thing...

Practice everything at the speed you're capable of playing it.

If you nail it slowly, you just have to speed it up.

Feel free to contact me at den@guitarin1hour. I would love to hear from you.

To check out courses around this playbook go to: **https://LearningGuitarSecrets.com**

Den López

Made in the USA
Las Vegas, NV
18 March 2024

ISBN 9798392607365

9 798392 607365

9000

Teacher Created Materials

TCM 2333

A Guide for Using
Across Five Aprils
in the Classroom

- Curriculum Connections
- Vocabulary
- Unit Tests
- Critical Thinking

Teacher Created Materials, Inc.

Literature Units

PRIMARY

TCM2347—Alexander and the Terrible, Horrible,
No Good, Very Bad Day
TCM0818—Amelia Bedelia
TCM0533—Arthur's Eyes
TCM2593—Bedtime for Frances
TCM2625—Brown Bear, Brown Bear, What Do You See?
TCM2630—Caps for Sale
TCM0540—The Cat in the Hat
TCM2336—The Clifford Series
TCM3004—Corduroy Series
TCM2642—The Courage of Sarah Noble
TCM3152—Curious George Series
TCM2640—Frog and Toad Are Friends
TCM2084—The Great Kapok Tree
(Rain Forest/Environment)
TCM0531—If You Give a Mouse a Cookie
and If You Give a Moose a Muffin
TCM2631—Ira Sleeps Over
TCM0536—Johnny Appleseed
(Apples/Westward Movement)
TCM0817—Jumanji
TCM0538—Madeline *(French)*
TCM2641—Miss Nelson is Missing
TCM2627—The Mitten
TCM0535—Molly's Pilgrim *(Immigration)*
TCM2346—Nate the Great
TCM0769—Pocahontas *(Native American)*
TCM0543—The Polar Express *(Christmas)*
TCM3005—Stone Soup
TCM0436—Strega Nona *(Italian)*
TCM0568—Too Much Noise
TCM2335—The Very Hungry Caterpillar
TCM0525—Where the Wild Things Are

THE MAGIC SCHOOL BUS®
SCIENCE/LITERATURE UNITS

TCM0544—Inside the Earth
TCM0815—Inside the Human Body
TCM2082—Electric Field Trip
TCM2085—On the Ocean Floor
TCM2086—Lost in the Solar System
TCM2087—In the Time of the Dinosaurs
TCM2088—At the Waterworks
TCM2089—Inside a Hurricane
TCM2137—Inside a Beehive

INTERMEDIATE

TCM0437—The Best Christmas Pageant Ever
TCM0410—The Black Pearl *(Mexican)*
TCM2339—The Borrowers
TCM2338—Boxcar Children:
Surprise Island
TCM0534—Bunnicula
TCM0528—By the Great Horn Spoon! *(Gold Rush)*
TCM0445—Caddie Woodlawn *(Westward Movement)*
TCM0420—Charlie & the Chocolate Factory
TCM0435—Charlotte's Web *(Friends/Spiders)*
TCM2337—The Chocolate Touch
TCM0419—The Cricket in Times Square
TCM0541—Dear Mr. Henshaw
TCM2632—The Enormous Egg
TCM0428—Farmer Boy
TCM2345—Freckle Juice
TCM2343—The Great Gilly Hopkins
TCM2133—Harriet the Spy
TCM0816—How to Eat Fried Worms
TCM2136—The Hundred Dresses
TCM0417—In the Year of the Boar & Jackie
Robinson *(Chinese American)*
TCM0412—Island of the Blue
Dolphins *(Native American)*
TCM0441—James and the Giant Peach *(Insects)*
TCM0409—The Lion, the Witch and the
Wardrobe *(English)*
TCM0522—Little House in the Big Woods
(Westward Movement)
TCM0539—Little House on the Prairie
(Westward Movement)
TCM0819—Matilda
TCM3064—Missing May
TCM2624—Misty of Chincoteague
TCM0529—The Mouse and the Motorcycle
TCM0549—Mr. Popper's Penguins
TCM0523—Mrs. Frisby and the Rats of NIMH
TCM2507—My Brother Sam is Dead
TCM3157—My Father's Dragon
TCM0424—Number the Stars *(Holocaust)*
TCM0425—Sarah, Plain and Tall *and* Journey
TCM0414—The Secret Garden *(English)*
TCM0402—The Sign of the Beaver
(Early & Native American)
TCM0567—Stone Fox
TCM2628—Stuart Little
TCM0526—Tales of a Fourth Grade Nothing
TCM2629—The Velveteen Rabbit
TCM2334—The War with Grandpa
TCM0403—A Wrinkle in Time

CHALLENGING

TCM2333—Across Five Aprils *(Civil War)*
TCM0444—Adam of the Road *(Medieval English)*
TCM0564—The Adventures of Huckleberry Finn
TCM2637—The Adventures of Tom Sawyer
TCM0559—Anne Frank: The Diary of a
Young Girl *(Holocaust)*
TCM0438—Anne of Green Gables *(Canadian)*
TCM0616—The Big Wave *(Japanese)*
TCM0416—The Black Stallion
TCM0401—Bridge to Terabithia
TCM3153—Bud, Not Buddy *(Depression)*
TCM0930—Call It Courage *(Polynesian)*
TCM0446—The Call of the Wild *(Wolves)*
TCM2139—Catherine, Called Birdy
TCM0447—The Cay *(African American)*
TCM0565—Charley Skedaddle *(Civil War)*
TCM0434—A Christmas Carol *(English)*
TCM0423—D'Aulaires' Book of Greek Myths
TCM0422—Dicey's Song
TCM0814—Dragon's Gate *(Chinese American)*
TCM3006—The Egypt Game *(Ancient Egyptian)*
TCM0448—From the Mixed-up Files of Mrs.
Basil E. Frankweiler
TCM2634—The Gift of the Magi and Other Stories
TCM0542—The Giver
TCM0442—The Golden Goblet *(Ancient Egyptian)*
TCM0449—Hatchet *(Survival)*
TCM0405—The Hobbit
TCM2650—Holes
TCM0520—I Heard the Owl Call My Name
(Native American)
TCM0521—The Incredible Journey *(Canadian)*
TCM0415—The Indian in the Cupboard
TCM0440—Johnny Tremain *(Revolutionary War)*
TCM0430—Journey to Topaz
(Japanese American/WWII)
TCM0418—Julie of the Wolves *(Wolves)*
TCM0537—Maniac Magee
TCM2517—The Master Puppeteer *(Ancient Japan)*
TCM3154—My Louisiana Sky
TCM3061—My Side of the Mountain
TCM2633—The Odyssey
TCM0427—Old Yeller
TCM0426—On My Honor
TCM2623—Out of the Dust *(Great Depression)*
TCM0406—The Outsiders
TCM0407—The Pearl *(Mexican)*
TCM0524—The People Could Fly *(African America)*
TCM0431—The Phantom Tollbooth
TCM3151—The Red Badge of Courage *(Civil War)*
TCM0443—The Red Pony
TCM0413—Rifles for Watie *(Native American/Civil)*
TCM0439—Roll of Thunder, Hear My Cry
(African American)
TCM2135—Romeo and Juliet *(English)*
TCM0411—Shadow of a Bull *(Spanish)*
TCM0566—Shiloh
TCM0432—Sing Down the Moon *(Native American)*
TCM0530—Sounder *(African American)*
TCM2588—SOS Titanic
TCM0532—Summer of the Swans
TCM2626—To Kill a Mockingbird
TCM0408—Tuck Everlasting
TCM2348—The View from Saturday
TCM3155—The Watsons Go to Birmingham–1963
TCM0400—Where the Red Fern Grows
TCM0920—The Whipping Boy
TCM0404—The Witch of Blackbird Pond
(Colonial America)
TCM3156—A Year Down Yonder
TCM2636—The Yearling

Quality Resource Books from **Teacher Created Materials**

A600 12/01